Who Is
the Dalai Lama?

by Dana Meachen Rau

illustrated by Dede Putra

Penguin Workshop
An Imprint of Penguin Random House

For all who spread peace, compassion,
humor, and happiness—DMR

Dedicated to my mom—DP

PENGUIN WORKSHOP
Penguin Young Readers Group
An Imprint of Penguin Random House LLC

Text copyright © 2018 by Dana Meachen Rau. Illustrations copyright © 2018 by
Penguin Random House LLC. All rights reserved. Published by Penguin Workshop,
an imprint of Penguin Random House LLC, 345 Hudson Street, New York,
New York 10014. PENGUIN and PENGUIN WORKSHOP are trademarks
of Penguin Books Ltd. WHO HQ & Design is a registered trademark of
Penguin Random House LLC. Printed in the USA.

Library of Congress Cataloging-in-Publication Data is available.

ISBN 9781101995549 (paperback)   10 9 8 7 6 5 4 3 2 1
ISBN 9781524786137 (library binding)   10 9 8 7 6 5 4 3 2 1

Contents

Who Is the Dalai Lama?

February 22, 1940, was a busy day at the Potala, a grand, thousand-room palace high in the mountains of Tibet. Early in the morning, guests started to fill the main assembly hall. They were waiting for their leader to arrive.

Once the hall was full, the crowd grew quiet. A little boy, dressed in golden robes,

entered. Horn and trumpet blasts greeted him. He crossed the room on a white carpet that had been rolled out especially for him to a jeweled throne. It was called the Lion Throne because of the eight lions carved into the wooden base of the tall, cushioned chair. The throne was the seat of the Dalai Lama (say: DAHL-eye LAH-muh), a name given to the political and religious leader of the country of Tibet.

The young Dalai Lama needed some help climbing up the steps to his throne. He sat cross-legged on the seat and watched the ceremonies, dances, and readings. Many gifts were set out for the boy—a music box, the tusk of an elephant, expensive fabrics, parakeets, a tricycle, and even a brick of gold! Holy men, government officials, and the others in attendance, in a sign of respect, bowed so low before him that they were lying on the floor. "I found that funny," he later said. The Dalai Lama is known for his sense of humor.

But it was especially funny to him that the adults were acting this way. After all, he was only four years old!

As he grew, that young boy on the Lion Throne began to understand why that day was so special.

As Tibet's Fourteenth Dalai Lama, he would face joyful times and difficult times. He would grow in wisdom. And he would become caring and strong.

But on his enthronement day, he had no idea what lay ahead for himself and for the people of Tibet. Along with the many gifts the little boy received, he also held an adventurous future in his hands.

CHAPTER 1
Little Lhamo

Diki Tsering woke very early on July 6, 1935. She went out behind her mud-and-stone house in Taktser, Tibet, to the barn. There, among the animals, she gave birth to her son Lhamo (say: LAM-oh). He didn't cry. His eyes were open wide.

Lhamo's mother, Diki, and father, Choekyong Tsering, already had four children—their daughter, Dolma, and three sons named Norbu, Gyalo, and Lobsang. There wasn't much furniture in their six-room house. The children didn't have their own beds. The family mostly gathered in the kitchen, especially during cold Tibetan winters, to keep warm by the fire.

They practiced Tibetan Buddhism, a religion that was very important to them and to all Tibetans. So their house also had a prayer room, where the family left offerings of food and flowers at a small altar.

Taktser, a small village in the northeastern province of Amdo, was on a hill with a view of a wide valley. The land and the weather weren't good for farming, but families, including Lhamo's, still tried their best to grow crops.

Buddhism

Buddhism is a religion founded by Siddhartha Gautama. This prince lived sometime between the sixth and fourth centuries BC in northern India. He was known as Buddha.

Buddha gave up a royal life to search for enlightenment, or Nirvana. Enlightenment is complete happiness and goodness and an end to suffering. Buddha taught others how to find this peace within themselves. After Buddha died, his followers continued to practice his lessons. Buddhism became a major religion that spread into Tibet in the seventh century AD.

In Tibetan Buddhism, *lamas* are important teachers who guide people toward enlightenment. There are between ten and twenty million Tibetan Buddhists in the world today.

His family grew barley, buckwheat, and potatoes. Before Lhamo was born, the village suffered from a long drought. No rain had fallen in years, and hail had destroyed the plants in the fields. Many villagers were starving.

Once Lhamo could walk, he followed his mother around the farm as she did her chores. He held the bowl as she milked the *dzomos* (say: ZHO-mohs)—animals that are a cross between yaks and cows. Little Lhamo was playful.

When his mother carried him on her shoulders, he pulled at her ears to show her which way to go. When she sent him to gather eggs from the chickens, she discovered him clucking and sitting with the hens in their nests.

The Tsering family farm also had yaks, sheep, goats, and horses. Lhamo's father especially loved the horses. But he was often angry and harsh with his children. Lhamo's mother, on the other hand, was gentle and kind. Lhamo later said, "My first teacher of compassion was my mother."

Compassion means wanting to help someone who is suffering, hurt, or in trouble. Lhamo saw compassion in the way his mother treated him and the way she shared what she could with the needy people in their village.

One of Lhamo's favorite games was to pack up his clothes and pretend to go on trips. He straddled the windowsill, pretending to ride a horse. His mother asked him where he was going. He said he was headed to Lhasa, the capital city of Tibet.

Lhamo didn't know that more than a thousand miles away, in Lhasa, something important was happening. In December 1933, the Thirteenth Dalai Lama had died. So Tibet had been without a leader for two years. Government officials and religious leaders had started the search to find the next Dalai Lama.

What Is a Dalai Lama?

Tibetan Buddhism is divided into groups. The most powerful one is called the *Gelugpa*, or Yellow Hat school. The most important person in this school is called the Dalai Lama. (*Dalai* is from the word for "ocean," and *lama* means "teacher.") He is considered the political and religious leader of Tibet.

The first Dalai Lama lived in the 1400s. Throughout history, there have been fourteen Dalai Lamas. Tibetan Buddhists believe that when a Dalai Lama dies, he is born back into the world— or reincarnated—into another body, so he can continue to lead the Tibetan people and share his message of compassion.

Gendün Druppa, the first Dalai Lama

CHAPTER 2
Searching for Signs

When the Thirteenth Dalai Lama died in 1933, Buddhist monks displayed his body so that Tibetans could visit and offer their respects to him. The monks placed the Dalai Lama so that his head tilted toward the south. But one

morning, they found his face had turned toward the northeast! When it happened a second time, the monks thought it might be a sign.

They believed that the Dalai Lama's soul would be reincarnated (reborn) in the body of a new person. Perhaps this was a sign that their next leader would be found living in a region to the northeast.

Reting Rinpoche

Monks all over Tibet were on the lookout for the next Dalai Lama. Reting Rinpoche (say: RIHN-poh-CHAY), who was acting as Tibet's temporary leader, went to look for signs himself. He journeyed to a lake that was thought to have special powers. For centuries, Tibetans had visited the lake hoping to see inspiring visions. While there, Reting Rinpoche closed his eyes and thought deeply. When he opened his eyes, he saw three Tibetan letters rise out of the water—*Ah*, *Ka*, and *Ma*. He also saw a vision of a three-story monastery with a blue-and-gold roof and a small house on a hill. He hoped that these signs would lead him to the next Dalai Lama.

In late 1936, search parties made up of monks and government members set out from Lhasa and headed east.

One group traveled to the province of Amdo, because *Ah* was one of the letters Reting Rinpoche saw on the lake. It was a difficult trek on horseback over rough land and through harsh snow.

Monasteries

Monasteries were the centers of religious life in Tibet. Parents sent their young sons, often between the ages of six and twelve, to the monasteries. There, they learned from teachers, called lamas, and became monks. Around the time Lhamo was born, more than half of Tibetan boys and men were monks.

At the monasteries, boys had to shave their heads and wear red and yellow robes. They studied sacred Buddhist books and learned to chant and pray. They also learned how to meditate—to focus quietly in their minds. When students were ready, they took vows to become monks, living simply and serving others at the monastery and in their communities for the rest of their lives.

After a few months, the men from Lhasa reached Amdo and were pleased with what they saw. The monastery in Amdo had three floors and a blue-and-gold roof, just like in the vision! They spent some time there, making a list of possible boys that might be the next Dalai Lama.

They interviewed and tested many children on the list, but they all failed. There was only one name left.

The search party set out from the monastery, following a road to a small house that also matched the one Reting Rinpoche had described in his vision. They were hoping that the Thirteenth Dalai Lama's soul had been reborn into the young boy who lived inside. It was Lhamo's house.

It was very snowy on the day the group arrived. The men pretended to be travelers and asked for shelter. Diki, with her compassionate spirit, welcomed them; fed them tea, bread, and dried meat; and let them stay overnight. The family did not know that their visitors were on a mission to find the Dalai Lama.

A few weeks later, the men returned. When Khetsang Rinpoche, a high-ranking lama, sat down in their kitchen, Lhamo jumped onto his lap. "I recognized many of them," he later said, "although I had never met them." Two-and-a-half-year-old Lhamo grabbed at the prayer beads around Khetsang's neck. He wanted them. The beads had belonged to the previous Dalai Lama.

Khetsang saw this as a sign that Lhamo might be the Thirteenth Dalai Lama's reincarnation.

But Khetsang and his men needed to test Lhamo to be sure. They showed him different  objects, including prayer beads and small drums. Some of the items had belonged to the Thirteenth Dalai Lama, while the others did not. The men waited. If Lhamo did indeed have the soul of the last Dalai Lama, he would recognize the correct items as his own. Lhamo chose all the right ones. Later, he said, "This may seem mysterious and even magical for most people, but when I saw those objects what I felt was nothing extraordinary. It was as if I was looking at things I was accustomed to."

The visitors finally told Lhamo's parents that they were, in fact, searching for the Fourteenth

Dalai Lama. If their son was chosen, it would be a huge honor for Lhamo's family. The holy men said that they were considering a few boys. But really, they had already decided that Lhamo was the reborn leader of Tibet.

When the search party left the next morning, Lhamo cried. He wanted to go with them! But Lhamo was still too young. He needed to stay with his family. Only a few years later, after Lhamo had turned four years old, was he ready to leave for Lhasa.

CHAPTER 3
Journey to the Throne

A large caravan (a group of travelers) set out from the Amdo region in July 1939 for the three-month journey to Lhasa. It was made up of about fifty people, including Lhamo's parents, his brothers Gyalo and Lobsang, lots of supplies, and more than three hundred yaks, camels, horses, and mules. There were no cars to ride in or roads to follow. They trekked along rough caravan routes, on foot or on the backs of the animals, through grasslands, forests, and mountains. Every night, they slept in large tents made from yak hair.

Roof of the World

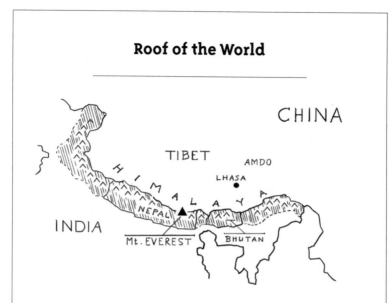

Most of Tibet is a plateau—a high, flat area of land—on the continent of Asia. Tibet's longest borders are with Nepal and India. It is ringed by mountains. The snow-capped Himalayas, including Mount Everest, which rises 29,028 feet above sea level, form its southern border. Because Tibet has some of the highest land on Earth, it's often called the Roof of the World.

Lhamo rode in a palanquin (say: pal-uhn-KEEN), a fancy box, like a small room, that was made of yellow fabric and carried by horses. Out the palanquin's windows, he saw sights he had never seen before. He passed lakes, mountains, valleys, plains, and lots of animals: herds of wild yaks, flocks of geese, and wild donkeys. Lhamo was sometimes a troublemaker on the trip. When he was bored, he nagged and fought with his brother, Lobsang, who rode along with him.

Tibetan officials formally announced that the boy coming to the capital was the next Dalai Lama. Hundreds of people began lining the caravan's path as it got closer to Lhasa. They were eager to meet Lhamo.

The caravan stopped at a monastery about three days away from Lhasa. There, Reting Rinpoche welcomed him. Even though Lhamo was so young, he was already behaving like a holy leader, blessing the many people who came to see him. The group grew as Reting and more

monks joined the caravan. For the last part of the journey, Lhamo rode in an even fancier palanquin, no longer carried by horses, but carried on the shoulders of eight men.

As their procession entered the city on October 8, 1939, crowds gathered. It was hard for them to even get through the streets!

The Tibetans held sticks of sweet-smelling incense and held out white scarves to show their respect.

Some people cried with happiness. The last Dalai Lama had died almost six years earlier, and they were filled with joy at the sight of this little boy who would be their next religious and political leader.

Lhamo was then brought to a temple in the middle of the city. His hair was shaved off, like all the other monks. He was also given his new name. Lhamo would now be known as: Jamphel Ngawang Lobsang

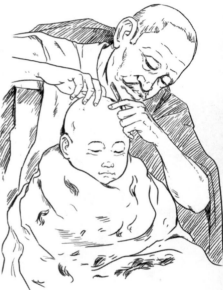

Yeshe Tenzin Gyatso, or just Tenzin Gyatso (say: TEHN-zihn gee-OT-soh) for short. But each of his many names had a special meaning. They made it clear to the Tibetan people that this little

boy was holy, a good speaker, compassionate, and had an ocean of wisdom.

After three long months of rough travel, the Tsering family was brought to a beautiful place to rest—the Norbulingka Palace, one of two palaces in the city. They were treated like royalty. Lhamo, who was still only four years old, didn't seem to understand what all the attention was about.

The Norbulingka Palace

The palace was much fancier than the small village he knew so well. Curious and playful, he explored his new home. One day, his mother found him opening many of the trunks he had found in his rooms. The belongings of the Thirteenth Dalai Lama had been stored inside. He said he was looking for his teeth! Finally, he found the box he had been looking for. When he and his mother opened it, they found the dentures of the previous Dalai Lama! Lhamo was just a little boy, but those around him saw this as further proof that he was truly the next leader of Tibet.

Lhamo lived in the Norbulingka Palace for four months. Then, on February 21, his servants woke him early. Like any child, he complained that he wanted to sleep longer. But they told him it was an important day. He would be moving into the Potala Palace.

Once again, the young boy found himself as part of a grand procession, riding in a golden palanquin, this time from one palace to another.

Servants walked first, carrying his household items, such as food, pots and pans, clothing, and bedsheets. The parade also included important government members and religious leaders.

Everyone wore colorful clothing, and everything was decorated in bright colors, even the horses. Thousands of Tibetans lined the route between the palaces dressed in their finest clothes, too. Songs and incense filled the air.

The next day, February 22, 1940, was enthronement day—the day the new Dalai Lama would sit on the throne of Tibet for the first time. The main assembly hall at the Potala Palace was packed with people. The crowd watched the four-year-old boy climb onto the Lion Throne. He sat still all day, listening to the prayers, watching dancers, and enjoying the ceremonies. Then they feasted—and the young Dalai Lama was served first.

At the end of the day, he was led to his rooms at the Potala Palace. Such a little boy needed rest for the many busy days ahead. Now that it was official, he also needed to be trained to take on his role as the Fourteenth Dalai Lama.

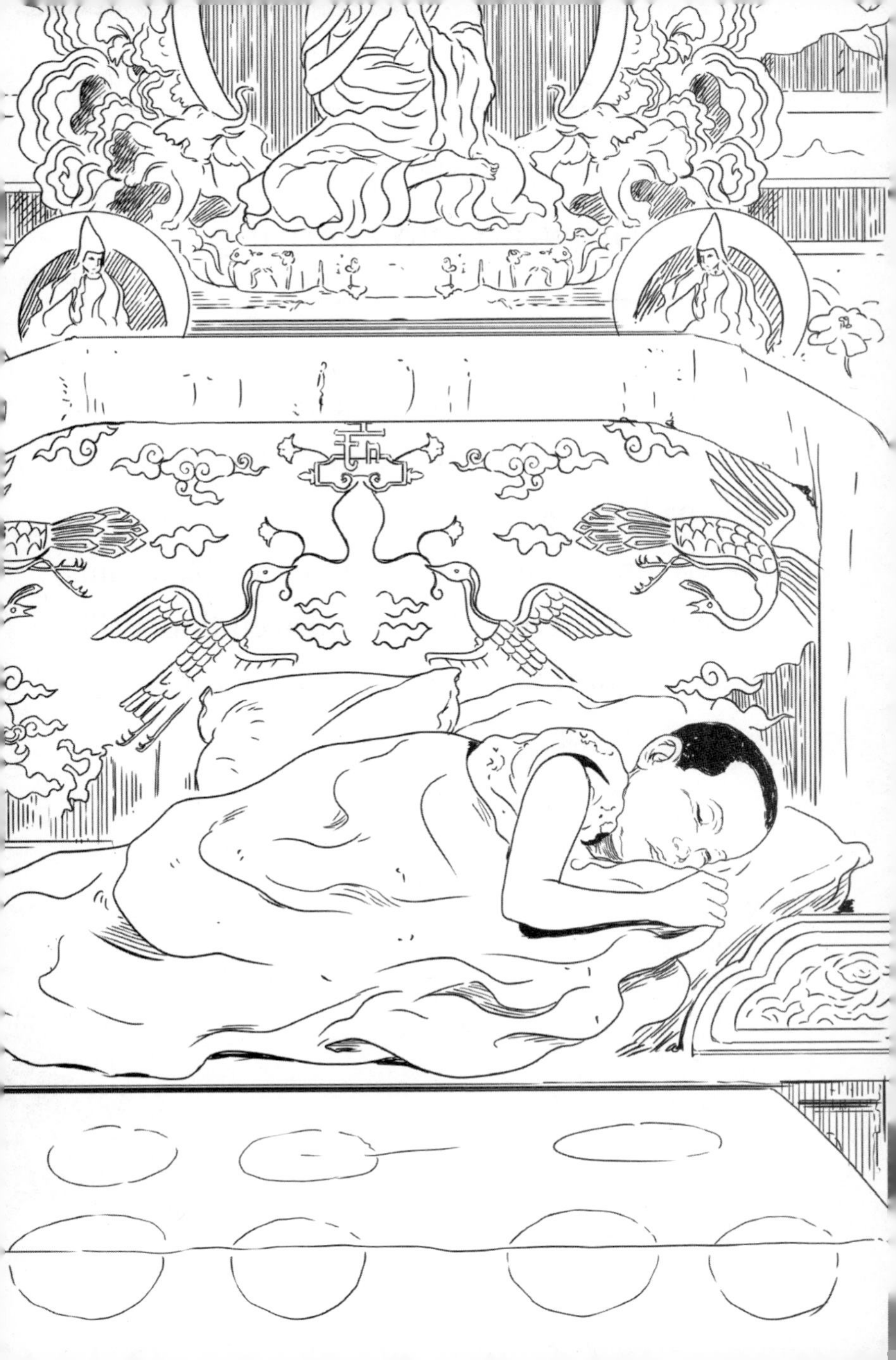

CHAPTER 4
Growing and Learning

The huge Potala Palace stood high on a hill overlooking Lhasa. From the city below, its slanted walls made it look even taller than it really was. Chapels, prayer halls, offices, libraries, bedrooms, and even a dungeon filled its thirteen floors. The palace had more than a thousand rooms!

The Dalai Lama's rooms were high in the palace and often dark and smoky from the oil lamps. He wasn't allowed to have friends his own age, and he was lonely. He would watch the children in the city below through a telescope and wonder why he couldn't join them. So he became friends with the palace servants. He was very close to the monk in charge of his meals, a man he called Ponpo. Ponpo was as kind and compassionate as the Dalai Lama's mother had been. He played with the Dalai Lama and even gave him lumps of sugar as a treat.

The Dalai Lama's brother Lobsang, who was two years older, was allowed to live with him at the Potala. And the Tibetan government provided a house for his family nearby. The Dalai Lama visited them there. Because Buddhism taught that one should not kill any living thing, the Dalai Lama and the monks at the palace didn't eat food from animals. But at his parents' house, the Dalai Lama would sneak fish, eggs, and pork.

He didn't worry about getting in trouble because, after all, he was the Dalai Lama!

At such a young age, the Dalai Lama wasn't yet ready to rule Tibet. First Reting Rinpoche and then Taktra Rinpoche did that. But when the

Taktra Rinpoche

Dalai Lama turned six, he was old enough to start training as a Buddhist monk. Tutors taught the Dalai Lama and Lobsang lessons together. The boys learned to read and write. And they had to memorize religious texts. They learned how to meditate in silence and reflect on all they had learned.

The tutors felt that the Dalai Lama was a good student. But the young boy often wished he could be playing instead of studying. He and Lobsang liked to explore all the rooms in the palace.

They were filled with priceless gold and silver objects, painted scrolls, books, shoes, swords, weapons, and armor. The Dalai Lama especially liked tinkering with music boxes and clocks to see how they worked. He would take them apart and put them back together again.

Even though he was still very young, everyone called him His Holiness. They spoke formally to him, bowed low, and even lay down on the ground in front of him. When he did something wrong, the monks didn't want to punish him. He was their leader! So the tutors would often punish poor Lobsang instead.

The Dalai Lama spent winters in the Potala Palace. In summers, he returned to the Norbulingka. He liked the summer palace so much more! It was smaller and had only about 350 rooms instead of 1,000. *Norbulingka* means "jeweled garden." And the Dalai Lama played in its gardens of flowers and fruit trees. He took his

small boat out onto the pond and dropped food to the fish while the adults watched him from shore.

When the Dalai Lama turned eight, his brother Lobsang left the palace to go to another school. They saw each other for visits, but it wasn't the same. "I remember, standing at the window watching, my heart full of sorrow, as he disappeared into the distance," the Dalai Lama said.

The Potala Palace Today

The Potala Palace rises high on a hill in Lhasa. The fifth Dalai Lama began building it in 1645 on the site of a previous seventh century palace. It has a golden roof and two main parts—the Red Palace and the White Palace. The Red is a holy site and used for prayer and the study of Buddhism. The White contains many government offices.

The Potala holds many artifacts from Tibetan history and religion. Its rooms are decorated with gold and gems. They are filled with statues, paintings, and sculptures. Murals painted on the walls tell the story of Tibet.

There are no escalators or elevators up to the palace. Visitors climb more than four hundred steps to get there!

The Tsering family was changing. The Dalai Lama's brother Norbu was a busy monk, Lobsang and Gyalo were off at school, and his sister Dolma had moved back in with the family. His parents had another daughter, Jetsun Pema, and another son, Tendzin Choegyal. His father often came to the palace for morning tea, so the Dalai Lama saw him often. But sadly, in 1947, when he was about twelve years old, his father died. According to custom, the family prayed for forty-nine days and gave away everything that belonged to him.

As the Dalai Lama reached his teenage years, he still lived a sheltered life in the palace, but he was becoming more curious about the world outside Tibet. He heard that a mountain climber from Austria, named Heinrich Harrer, was visiting Tibet. The Dalai Lama wanted to meet this daring explorer, so he asked him to visit the palace. Harrer tutored him in history, science,

Heinrich Harrer

and geography. He was happy to answer many of the Dalai Lama's curious questions.

The Tibetans had first seen him as a little boy arriving in Lhasa. But as the Dalai Lama grew older, he was learning how to become a leader.

He watched and learned from his government advisors at the palace. His studies with the monks taught him the values of Buddhism. And his time alone and sheltered from others had trained him to think deeply and meditate on ideas of leadership and compassion. All these things were preparing him to guide the people of Tibet. The Dalai Lama knew his people expected a lot from him. He wanted to do great things for them, too.

CHAPTER 5
A Violent Chinese Takeover

In 1949, the Chinese Communist Party took over the government of China. Communists believe that the community, not the individual, should have control over how people live and work.

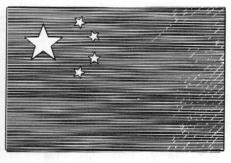

Flag of the People's Republic of China

China bordered Tibet on the north and east. Tibetans had once been ruled by China, but since the early 1900s, they had ruled themselves. The Chinese Communist leader Mao Tse-tung (say: MOU tsuh-TOONG) wanted to control Tibet once again.

Mao Tse-tung (1893–1976)

Mao was born in 1893 to a farming family in China. He liked the Communist idea of government control. And he helped establish the Chinese Communist Party.

In 1949, the Chinese Communist Party took over the government, and Mao became the chairman of the People's Republic of China. His government took over land, farming, and the industries of the country. This led to food shortages and starvation for many Chinese people. He wanted to eliminate all of China's old ways. So he destroyed books and works of art.

He closed schools that did not support Communist ideas. Those who didn't agree with him were put in prison or killed.

The Communists of China thought of Mao as a national hero who helped China become more modern. Others saw him as a terrible dictator who was responsible for the deaths of millions of Chinese citizens.

The Chinese and Tibetans have very different cultures. They don't speak or write the same languages. The Communist Chinese didn't like Tibet's religion or traditions. They wanted Tibetans to change their ways and become Communists, too.

The Chinese government sent soldiers over the border into Tibet. These military troops were called the People's Liberation Army (PLA). *Liberation* means freedom. The Chinese believed that they were going to liberate, or free, Tibet from its old ways.

But the Tibetans didn't want to change. Their religion—Buddhism—taught nonviolence, which meant that most Tibetans believed in peace, not in fighting. Some Tibetans did try to fight back against the invading PLA. But their soldiers were no match for China's army. The PLA made its way across Tibet, moving closer to Lhasa.

Tibet's government officials were worried. They needed to have a strong leader to unite the country against the Chinese. They wondered if the Dalai Lama was ready to take on his role as Tibet's political leader. The Dalai Lama was nervous, too. He was only fifteen years old. But one of the wise religious leaders said, "His time has come." So on November 17, 1950, the teenage lama was given full responsibility to lead Tibet.

Six months later, the Chinese government forced the Tibetan government to sign an agreement saying that Tibet was a part of China.

Tibetan leaders signing the Seventeen-Point Agreement

The document said that the Chinese were still going to allow Tibet to govern itself. The Dalai Lama hoped the agreement would stop the violence of the PLA against his people.

In 1954, Mao Tse-tung invited the Dalai Lama to China. During the almost yearlong visit,

Mao and the Dalai Lama had public and private meetings. The Dalai Lama was polite and willing

to listen. He was impressed by some of the things Mao had done to help modernize China. But he also saw the poor living conditions of the people in China's countryside. Near the end of the trip, Mao said, "Religion is poison." This scared the Dalai Lama. The Buddhist religion was the center of Tibetan culture.

As the Dalai Lama passed through regions of Tibet on his way home, including the village where he had been born, he saw how poorly his own people were living under Chinese control. The Chinese weren't keeping their promise to let Tibet govern itself. PLA troops kept moving in. They took land away from the people. They tore down monasteries. They forced the Tibetans to join the army or work on new building programs. They took children away to China to attend Communist schools there. They were trying to completely destroy Tibet's culture and religion.

Even though most Tibetans were peaceful
people, many started fighting back. This made
the Chinese soldiers even more violent. Besides
battles on the ground and on horseback, the
Chinese bombed eastern areas from the sky.
Tibetans fled from the countryside to Lhasa for
safety. The population of the capital grew.

In March 1959, when the Dalai Lama was twenty-three, two Chinese soldiers came to visit him at the temple in Lhasa. They invited him to a performance at the Chinese army's headquarters on March 10. They told him he had to come alone. He couldn't bring any Tibetan soldiers or bodyguards with him. The Dalai Lama planned to go to the performance, but many of his advisors wondered if it was a trap. Without soldiers or bodyguards with him, the Dalai Lama could be kidnapped, or worse.

Early on the morning of March 10, he heard shouting outside his palace. The Tibetan people had surrounded the Norbulingka. They didn't want him to go near the Chinese army's headquarters. To protect him, they had brought along sticks, knives, and anything they could use against the Chinese.

The Dalai Lama prayed. He decided not to leave the palace. He didn't want fighting in Lhasa's streets. He worried about what might happen next.

The Tibetan crowd around the Norbulingka grew to about three hundred thousand people, including children and even monks who were willing to fight and die for the Dalai Lama. The Chinese aimed cannons at the palace. Both sides were getting ready for war.

The Dalai Lama's advisors wanted to keep him safe. If he was killed, the Chinese would surely take over Tibet. So they told him he had to leave Lhasa. Protecting him meant protecting the future of Tibet.

CHAPTER 6
Escape to India

The morning of March 17, 1959, was much quieter than usual. Instead of clanging bells in the monasteries, the Tibetans in Lhasa were preparing for a battle. They hung anti-Chinese signs on the walls, covered up their windows, and handed out weapons to groups throughout the city.

A crowd still surrounded the Norbulingka Palace to protect their leader.

The Dalai Lama was unsure about leaving Lhasa. He knew that if he left Tibet, he might never be allowed to come back. When the Chinese started bombing the walls of the Norbulingka, the Dalai Lama finally knew it was time. He consulted a book filled with the teachings of Buddha. The page he read was about having courage. He thought about the courage he would need on the journey ahead.

When evening came, the Dalai Lama changed out of his monk's robes and dressed as a Tibetan soldier. He said goodbye to the people at the palace, including Ponpo, who had been with him since he first came to Lhasa almost twenty years earlier.

Late in the evening, he and others dressed as soldiers left through one of the Norbulingka's gates and made their way through the crowd.

No one recognized him. They crossed the Kyichu River in yak-skin boats. On the other side, they met the rest of their group, about one hundred in all, including government officials, his mother, and other members of his family.

They set off on horses, riding as fast as they could without stopping. It was freezing, windy, and dusty. By morning, they reached the Che-La mountain pass. At the top of the steep slope, the Dalai Lama looked back at Lhasa one last time.

The group was headed to India, on Tibet's southern border. India's prime minister, Jawaharlal Nehru, hadn't supported Tibet in the past. But maybe now that things were worse, he might be willing to help. The Dalai Lama hoped India would be a safe home for him and all the people fleeing the country with him.

Jawaharlal Nehru (1889–1964)

Jawaharlal Nehru was born in Allahabad, India.

He worked closely with Mahatma Gandhi to help free India from British rule. In 1947, India became independent, and Nehru was named its first prime minister.

As prime minister, he worked to give the people a voice in their government, to help the poor, and to promote education for all Indians.

The journey took two weeks with many obstacles along the way. The Tibetans had to cross the wide Tsangpo River and high mountain passes. The horses trudged over fresh snow, slippery ice, and thick mud. The weather often changed from bright sunlight to snowy blizzards, rainy downpours to swirling dust storms. The men's mustaches froze. They got frostbite. They even had to worry about wild wolves and bears. And they were always afraid that the Chinese would track them down.

Hundreds of armed warriors from south-eastern Tibet rode alongside the group to protect the Dalai Lama. Tibetan peasants and monks let them rest in their homes and monasteries along the route. They gave them food, clothing, and fresh horses.

During the journey, the Dalai Lama heard some bad news from the city of Lhasa.

After he had left, fighting between the Chinese and Tibetans lasted for three days. Gunfire, death, and sadness filled the streets of Lhasa. About eighty-six thousand Tibetans had been killed. The Chinese bombed the Norbulingka palace and monasteries. They were now in charge of Lhasa.

As they reached India, the group had more than tripled in size to about 350 people. On March 31, 1959, they were welcomed by Indian guards at the border. The Dalai Lama was sick with a high fever. He could hardly stay on his horse. But he had finally arrived in India. And Prime Minister Nehru was willing to help the Tibetans. The country of India would protect them.

Before the dramatic escape, people in the rest of the world didn't know much about Tibet. The country's high mountains and ancient traditions had kept it separate from outsiders. But word had spread about the Tibetan refugees. (Refugees are people who have to leave their homelands to escape war or other dangers.) A huge welcome waited for them in Tezpur, India. About two hundred journalists from newspapers all over the world had gathered there. They were eager to hear about Tibet and meet its twenty-three-year-old leader.

Prime Minister Nehru allowed the Dalai Lama and his people to settle in the misty hillside town of Dharamsala in northern India. The Dalai Lama thought it looked beautiful. It had more trees and rain than he had ever seen! "I was both happy and sad," he said about arriving in India. India had offered them a safe place to live. But he had left so many of his people behind.

CHAPTER 7
Hoping for Peace

The Dalai Lama and his people were now living in exile, which means that they had been forced to leave and could not return home. His new home in India was much smaller than the palaces of Tibet. He no longer had hundreds of servants, advisors, and monks surrounding him.

He wasn't carried around in a palanquin. He walked among his people. The Dalai Lama didn't miss the fancy ceremonies. Buddhist monks were expected to live simply, and now he did.

He was also glad to be more connected to the world outside Tibet. Now safely in India, he asked the United Nations (UN)—an international group that works for peace and human rights—for help protecting the Tibetan people from China. Human rights are the rights of all people—no matter what nation they are from, what religion they practice, or the color of their skin—to have equality, safety, fairness, and freedom. The UN spoke out in support of Tibetans and asked the Chinese government to respect these human rights.

During the Dalai Lama's first year in exile, about eighty thousand more Tibetans escaped to India and joined him. As their leader, he set up a government-in-exile. The government was based on both Buddhist ideas and democratic ones— such as the freedom to say what you want, freedom to believe what you want, and the freedom to meet together in groups.

He also wanted to protect the Tibetan traditions that the Chinese had tried to destroy. So, soon after he arrived, he established a school where students could learn Tibetan dance and music and a university where they could study Buddhist teachings.

While the Dalai Lama was setting up a "new" Tibet in India, things got even worse for those left behind. Mao Tse-tung made it his goal to get rid of all old ideas and customs. The Tibetan people had to change the way they dressed and even their language! Many people were killed. Many monasteries were torn down, and sacred texts and art were destroyed. The environment of Tibet was suffering, too. Forests were cut and the land polluted.

Over the next decades, the Dalai Lama grew from a young leader into a strong voice for his exiled nation. He visited many places in India and spoke about Tibet. He felt safe enough to leave India and spread the word in other Buddhist countries in Asia. In 1973, he visited European nations, including Italy, Switzerland, and Austria. And he visited the United States and Canada for the first time in 1979. He was helping the world open their eyes to the unfair treatment of Tibetans.

His Holiness the Dalai Lama greets Pope Paul VI

When Mao Tse-tung died in September 1976, the Dalai Lama looked for a sign of hope. It had been raining, but when it stopped, a rainbow appeared. "I was certain that it must be a good omen," the forty-one-year-old monk said.

And, sure enough, the Chinese invited the Dalai Lama back to Tibet! But they would not give Tibet independence from China. They wanted to keep control of the Tibetan people. So the Dalai Lama refused to return. He realized he could do more for Tibet by staying in India. He could keep Tibet's traditions safe and strong by remaining free of Chinese control.

By the end of the 1980s, Tibetans in Tibet had grown angry with the Chinese. They started to fight back. Lhasa once again became a battle zone, just like it had thirty years earlier when the Dalai Lama escaped. The fighting lasted more than a year.

The Dalai Lama was not looking for more battles with the Chinese. So he traveled, speaking about peace and hoping the rest of the world would listen. "Our struggle must remain nonviolent and free of hatred," he said. In 1987 and 1988, he visited the United States and Europe to share his peace plan with foreign governments.

The Dalai Lama presents his Five-Point Peace Plan in the European Parliament

This plan declared that Tibet should be a zone of peace and nonviolence. He wanted the Chinese to withdraw their soldiers. He wanted the rights of his people protected. He wanted Tibet's natural environment protected, too. The Dalai Lama's hope was to start conversations with Chinese leaders about their future together. He proposed that Tibet would be a province of China, but that Tibet would govern itself and be allowed to keep its own culture and religion. He wanted to create what he called The Middle Way—a compromise that would work for both Tibet and China.

But China wasn't willing to listen. They weren't interested in the Dalai Lama's plan. The Nobel Peace Prize committee, however, was very interested. In 1989, they awarded its international prize to His Holiness the Dalai Lama. The committee honored him with the award because of his compassion for the people of Tibet and his homeland. Instead of fighting against the Chinese government, he had chosen to look for a peaceful solution.

The Nobel Prizes

Alfred Nobel (1833–1896) was a wealthy Swedish inventor. When he died, he set aside money for prizes to be given out every year to people who made a difference in the world. There are five Nobel Prize categories: physics, chemistry, physiology or medicine, literature, and peace.

The Nobel Peace Prize Medal

According to Nobel's instructions, the Peace Prize is awarded each year to the person who has tried to create unity between nations, lessened the number of armies, and helped people come together in peace.

The Nobel Prizes were first given out in 1901 and are still awarded every year.

CHAPTER 8
Worldwide Celebrity

Winning the Nobel Peace Prize made the Dalai Lama famous all over the world. Everyone wanted to meet him. In just the few years after the award, he traveled to more than forty countries. He met government officials, religious leaders, professors, and journalists. The prize gave him a chance to give speeches to share his message of peace and compassion with more people than ever before.

The Dalai Lama meets with President Bill Clinton

Three Main Commitments

His Holiness, the Dalai Lama, feels very strongly about three main ideas and has pledged his life to following them. In his visits and speeches, he encourages others to do the same.

They are called his Three Main Commitments:

1. He believes that all human beings want the same things—to not suffer and to find happiness. He wants people to be compassionate, understanding, and forgiving.

2. He believes that people of different religions should respect one another's beliefs and traditions and work together peacefully.

3. He believes in protecting the lessons of Tibetan Buddhism and its message of peace and nonviolence.

The Tibetian symbol of peace

While he spread his message throughout the world, the people in Tibet were still suffering. The Chinese government controlled every part of the Tibetans' lives. They continued to erase Tibet's culture, language, and religion. If anyone was found with a picture of the Dalai Lama, they were arrested and thrown in jail. No one could speak out against the government. As more Chinese immigrants poured into Tibet, their population grew to outnumber the Tibetans. More Tibetans now lived safely outside Tibet than in it. The Dalai Lama was still working to reach a compromise with China. But the Chinese government would not agree to it.

As years passed, some Tibetan people began

to leave India. The Tibetans-in-exile spread to all parts of the globe. The Tibetan government, which calls itself the Central Tibetan Administration, held its first democratic elections in 2001. And Tibetan people all over the world elected their own officials.

Their "country" did not have specific borders, but it had a population of Tibetans who still believed in their homeland, no matter where they lived.

The Dalai Lama has written more than one hundred books, won awards from more than thirty countries, and holds prayer gatherings with hundreds of thousands of people. He speaks and writes about looking inward

to find happiness with one's self and also looking outward to help others throughout the world.

In 2011, the Dalai Lama made an announcement. He was stepping down as the political leader of Tibet, ending a more than 350-year-old tradition. He would still be the spiritual leader, but he felt that the time of one person holding all the political power in a country had passed. Instead, he felt Tibet should become a democracy, like so many other countries in the world. Tibet would be led by the Central Tibetan Administration, with leaders elected by the people.

The Dalai Lama has also said that he is not sure if his soul will be reborn into a new body after he dies. When he turns ninety, he will meet with religious leaders and Tibetans to decide if he should return. He will leave clear instructions for the search parties to identify his soul within the next young Tibetan.

Since the Dalai Lama turned eighty, he still has a lot of energy and continues to travel.

When he is home in Dharamsala, India, he wakes up at three o'clock in the morning and goes to bed at seven o'clock each night. He spends more than six hours a day praying and meditating.

While most Tibetans in Tibet don't remember a time when the Dalai Lama lived among them, he is always thinking of them. And he constantly reminds the world of the struggles happening there. He works hard to keep Tibetan culture alive in exile.

The Dalai Lama says: "We are all human, all seven billion of us. In this respect, we are all one hundred percent the same." He believes that no matter what country people are from, what language they speak, how much money they have, or which religion they practice—we are all human. We should have compassion for one another. Compassion, he says, is kind and gentle, but it is also powerful. He believes compassion is not just for the people you love, but also for your enemies. He even calls the Chinese people his "brothers and sisters."

Tibetan Freedom Concerts

People all over the world have helped the Dalai Lama spread his message. And some very famous musicians have participated in the Tibetan Freedom Concerts.

One hundred thousand people gathered at the first freedom concert in San Francisco's Golden Gate Park in 1996. In between performances by bands

including the Beastie Boys and the Red Hot Chili Peppers, fans heard from exiled Tibetans and other experts about why it was so important to know Tibet's story.

Since then, the concerts have been held in many cities all around the world. They have raised millions of dollars to support the exiled Tibetan community. And they have also encouraged many young people to stand up for human rights.

The Dalai Lama was a playful child in a country whose high, snow-capped mountains and peaceful way of life had kept it separate from the rest of the world. Once he was discovered to be the reincarnation of the Dalai Lama, he grew to become a leader who helped his country through

its most difficult times. His people worshipped him, even when he had to flee the country to survive. He went on to become a worldwide celebrity.

People admire the Dalai Lama because of his gentle, friendly, and compassionate manner.

Different religious leaders support him because he believes that everyone, no matter their religion, should work together to protect one another's human rights. Through all the attention, he is always humble. "I am no one special," he has said.

But he is very special. He is special to the Tibetans whom he has fought so hard to protect. He is a role model of compassion for all people. And he is still as friendly and curious as he was when he was a child. "I laugh often," he says. He uses his cheerful personality to spread his messages of hope and peace to people all over the world.

Timeline of the Dalai Lama's Life

1935 — Lhamo Thondup is born on July 6 to a farming family in the village of Taktser, Amdo Province, Tibet

1937 — The search party for the Fourteenth Dalai Lama visits Lhamo's home

1939 — Lhamo and his family take a three-month journey to Lhasa, the capital of Tibet, arriving on October 8

1940 — Lhamo is enthroned as the Dalai Lama at the Potala Palace on February 22

1950 — The Dalai Lama takes on full political power on November 17, after Chinese troops enter Tibet

1954–1955 — Visits China for peace talks with its leader, Mao Tse-tung

1959 — Flees Lhasa at night on March 17

— Arrives in India on March 31

1963 — Drafts a constitution for a more democratic government for the Tibetans in exile in India

1973 — Visits Western Europe for the first time

1987 — Visits the United States to announce his Five-Point Peace Plan to Congress in Washington, DC

1989 — Awarded the Nobel Peace Prize on December 10

2001 — Gives up some of his governing duties when Tibet holds its first democratic elections

2011 — Steps down as the political leader of Tibet and leaves governing to elected leaders

Timeline of the World

1939 — World War II begins

1943 — The Slinky spring toy is invented by engineer Richard James

1949 — The first NASCAR race is held in Charlotte, North Carolina

1950 — Charles M. Schulz's *Peanuts* comic strip first appears in newspapers

1959 — The Soviet space probe Luna 3 is the first to photograph the far side of the moon

1960 — American scientist Theodore H. Maiman builds the first laser

1970 — Earth Day is celebrated for the first time on April 22

1975 — Japanese mountain climber Junko Tabei becomes the first woman to reach the summit of Mt. Everest

1985 — American explorer Robert Ballard discovers the shipwreck of the *Titanic* in the Atlantic Ocean

1991 — Germans hiking along the Italy-Austria border discover a mummy of a man, now known as Ötzi, who was more than five thousand years old

2002 — Steve Fossett becomes the first person to fly around the world in a balloon alone, starting and ending in Australia

2012 — A huge hurricane, called Superstorm Sandy, hits the Caribbean and eastern United States and causes high winds, blizzard conditions, heavy rains, flooding, and massive destruction

Bibliography

*Books for young readers

Chhaya, Mayank. ***Dalai Lama: Man, Monk, Mystic***. New York: Doubleday, 2007.

The Dalai Lama. ***My Spiritual Journey: Personal Reflections, Teachings, and Talks***. Collected by Sofia Stril-Rever. Translated by Charlotte Mandell. New York: HarperOne, 2010.

The Dalai Lama. ***Beyond Religion: Ethics for a Whole World***. Boston: Houghton Mifflin Harcourt, 2011.

*Kimmel, Elizabeth Cody. ***Boy on the Lion Throne: The Childhood of the 14th Dalai Lama***. New York: Roaring Brook Press, 2008.

Mehrotra, Rajiv, ed. ***The Essential Dalai Lama: His Important Teachings***. New York: Viking, 2005.

Scorsese, Martin, director. ***Kundun***. Burbank, CA: Touchstone Pictures, 1997.

Talty, Stephan. ***Escape from the Land of Snows***. New York: Crown Publishers, 2011.

Tsering, Diki. ***Dalai Lama, My Son***. Edited by Khedroob Thondup. New York: Viking/Arkana, 2000.

Website

www.dalailama.com